OFFICIAL SQA PAST PAPERS WITH ANSWERS

STANDARD GRADE | GENERAL | CREDIT

BUSINESS MANAGEMENT

2006-2010

SQA

BrightRED PUBLISHING

First exam published in 2006.
Published by Bright Red Publishing Ltd, 6 Stafford Street, Edinburgh EH3 7AU
tel: 0131 220 5804 fax: 0131 220 6710 info@brightredpublishing.co.uk www.brightredpublishing.co.uk

ISBN 978-1-84948-081-9

A CIP Catalogue record for this book is available from the British Library.

Bright Red Publishing is grateful to the copyright holders, as credited on the final page of the book, for permission to use their material.
Every effort has been made to trace the copyright holders and to obtain their permission for the use of copyright material.
Bright Red Publishing will be happy to receive information allowing us to rectify any error or omission in future editions.

STANDARD GRADE | GENERAL

2006

[BLANK PAGE]

FOR OFFICIAL USE

G

	KU	DM
Total		

4200/402

NATIONAL QUALIFICATIONS 2006

FRIDAY, 12 MAY
10.20 AM – 11.35 AM

BUSINESS MANAGEMENT
STANDARD GRADE
General Level

Fill in these boxes and read what is printed below.

Full name of centre

Town

Forename(s)

Surname

Date of birth
Day Month Year

Scottish candidate number

Number of seat

1 Read each question carefully.

2 Attempt **all** the questions.

3 All answers are to be written in this answer book.

4 Do **not** write in the margins.

5 Before leaving the examination room you must give this book to the invigilator. If you do not, you may lose all the marks for this paper.

SCOTTISH QUALIFICATIONS AUTHORITY

DO NOT WRITE IN THIS MARGIN

Marks | KU | DM

1. Study the information below and then answer the questions that follow.

Samantha Hunter is a young entrepreneur who set up a cosmetics business "Forever Natural". She got a £10,000 loan to start up the business. She liked the idea of being her own boss and being the decision maker.

Adapted from website www.mybusiness.co.uk

(*a*) What is an entrepreneur?

____

____ 1

(*b*) Suggest **2 skills** or **qualities** which would be required by an entrepreneur like Samantha.

1 ____

2 ____ 2

(*c*) Identify the **4 factors of production** used in a business.

1 ____

2 ____

3 ____

4 ____ 4

(*d*) Name and describe the **type of business organisation** being operated by Samantha.

Type of business ______________________________

Description __________________________________

____

____ 2

DO NOT WRITE IN THIS MARGIN

Marks KU DM

1. (continued)

(*e*) Other than selling her products through shops, suggest **2 other methods** Samantha could use to sell her products. Justify your suggestions.

Method 1 ____________________

Justification ____________________

____

____

Method 2 ____________________

Justification ____________________

____

____________________ **4**

(*f*) Suggest **one** piece of **internal information** and **one** piece of **external information** which Samantha could find useful in running the business.

Internal ____________________

____

External ____________________

____________________ **2**

[Turn over

DO NOT WRITE IN THIS MARGIN

Marks	KU	DM

2. Study the information below and then answer the questions that follow.

Dowhill Farm and Country Fayre in Girvan has been praised by Scottish Ministers as a good example of diversification. Jimmy Crawford who owns the farm now runs a successful farm shop and restaurant and rents out three farm buildings as craft shop units. The farm received funding from the Government for this project.

Adapted from www.scotland.gov.uk/news/releases–12/8/2004

(*a*) Give **2 advantages** of diversification to **Jimmy Crawford**.

1 ______________________________

____

2 ______________________________

______________________________ **2**

(*b*) Suggest **one advantage** of diversification to the **local community**.

____

______________________________ **1**

(*c*) Other than funding from the Government, suggest and justify **one source of finance** for the business.

Suggestion ______________________________

____

Justification ______________________________

____

______________________________ **2**

DO NOT WRITE IN THIS MARGIN

Marks	KU	DM

2. (continued)

(*d*) Identify **2 stakeholders** in Dowhill Farm and Country Fayre and say how they can influence the business.

Stakeholder 1 ______________________________

Influence ______________________________

____

____

Stakeholder 2 ______________________________

Influence ______________________________

____

______________________________ **4**

(*e*) Jimmy Crawford is worried about rising costs, suggest **2** ways he could reduce his costs.

1 ______________________________

____

2 ______________________________

______________________________ **2**

[Turn over

DO NOT WRITE IN THIS MARGIN

Marks KU DM

3. Study the information below and then answer the questions that follow.

murray & murray

Murray & Murray is a partnership from Glenrothes producing designer kitchens. Their aim is to become Scotland's leading designer of kitchens but there is strong competition from other manufacturers.

The partnership makes use of skilled workers and the best materials to create individually produced kitchens to meet customer needs.

Adapted from article in Sunday Times 3 July 2005

(*a*) Give **2 advantages** of a partnership compared to a sole trader.

1 ______________________________

____

2 ______________________________

______________________________ **2**

(*b*) Suggest **2 ways** in which Murray & Murray can compete with other manufacturers.

1 ______________________________

____

2 ______________________________

______________________________ **2**

DO NOT WRITE IN THIS MARGIN

Marks | KU | DM

3. (continued)

(*c*) Name and describe the **method of production** used by Murray & Murray.

Method of Production ______________________________

Description ______________________________

____

______________________________ 2

(*d*) Give **2 reasons** why Murray & Murray use skilled workers.

1 ______________________________

____

2 ______________________________

______________________________ 2

(*e*) Suggest **one disadvantage** of using skilled workers.

____

______________________________ 1

[Turn over

DO NOT WRITE IN THIS MARGIN

Marks | KU | DM

4. Study the information below and then answer the questions that follow.

Innocent Drinks was started by three friends with no manufacturing experience. It makes smoothies with 100% pure fruit. Market research was first carried out by asking people their opinions. Today the product is sold in shops across the country.

People are very important to the company. New employees receive training. All employees are asked their opinions before decisions are made. To create a happy and motivated team of workers, every employee is treated to a snow boarding trip each year.

Adapted from website www.innocentdrinks.co.uk

(*a*) What **sector of industry** is manufacturing?

____ **1**

(*b*) Give **2 reasons** why Innocent Drinks carried out market research.

1 ____

____

2 ____

____ **2**

(*c*) Identify the **method** of market research used by Innocent Drinks.

____

____ **1**

DO NOT WRITE IN THIS MARGIN

Marks KU DM

4. (continued)

(*d*) Identify and describe the **style of management** used at Innocent Drinks.

Style of Management ______________________________

Description ______________________________

____

______________________________ **2**

(*e*) Name the **type of training** given to new employees.

______________________________ **1**

(*f*) Other than the snow boarding trip, suggest **2** ways Innocent Drinks could motivate employees.

1 ______________________________

____

2 ______________________________

______________________________ **2**

[Turn over

DO NOT WRITE IN THIS MARGIN

Marks KU DM

5. Study the information below and then answer the questions that follow.

ODEON CINEMAS

ODEON WEBSITE

Now showing: Disney - Chicken Little

Adapted from www.odeoncinemas.co.uk

(*a*) Identify **2 features** of a good website.

1 ______________________________

____

2 ______________________________

______________________________ **2**

(*b*) Suggest **2 advantages** to Odeon of having a website.

Advantage 1 ______________________________

____

____

Advantage 2 ______________________________

____

______________________________ **2**

(*c*) Identify **a problem** which customers might face when using a website.

____

______________________________ **1**

DO NOT WRITE IN THIS MARGIN

Marks | KU | DM

5. (continued)

(*d*) Suggest a **market segment** that Chicken Little is aimed at. **1**

(*e*) Suggest **a challenge** facing Odeon cinemas. **1**

(*f*) Identify and justify **2 methods of promotion** which Odeon cinemas could use.

Method 1

Justification

Method 2

Justification **4**

[Turn over for Question 6 on *Page twelve*

DO NOT WRITE IN THIS MARGIN

Marks KU DM

6. Study the Cash Budget below and then answer the questions that follow.

Cash Budget of Francisco Rodrigo
For 3 months January–March 2006

	January (£)	February (£)	March (£)
Opening Balance	500	2400	5000
Cash In			
Sales	13000	14700	15500
	13500	**17100**	**20500**
Cash Out			
Purchases	9000	10000	12000
Wages	700	700	700
Rent	800	800	800
Heating and Lighting	600	600	600
Purchase of Machine	0	0	8000
	11100	**12100**	**22100**
Closing Balance	2400	5000	(1600)

(*a*) (i) Which month had the **lowest sales**?

______________________________ **1**

(ii) Which month had the **highest total payments**?

______________________________ **1**

(*b*) Explain what has happened to the closing balance in March.

______________________________ **1**

(*c*) Suggest **2 changes** which could have been made to improve the closing balance in March.

1 ______________________________

____

2 ______________________________

______________________________ **2**

[*END OF QUESTION PAPER*]

STANDARD GRADE | CREDIT

2006

[BLANK PAGE]

C

4200/403

NATIONAL QUALIFICATIONS 2006

FRIDAY, 12 MAY
1.00 PM – 2.30 PM

BUSINESS MANAGEMENT
STANDARD GRADE
Credit Level

1 Read each question carefully.

2 Attempt **all** the questions.

3 All answers are to be written in the answer book provided.

DO NOT WRITE IN THIS MARGIN

KU DM

1.

Spanish fashion store Zara have introduced the concept of "fast fashion" to the high street. Twice a week lorries deliver garments to countries around Europe. The business uses a just-in-time approach to manufacturing and sales.

Zara has used "vertical integration" and now owns its entire manufacturing and distribution process.

Zara's shops use Point of Sale (POS) technology to communicate directly to head office in Spain and shop managers feed back customer information to help plan future designs. This keeps the designers in touch with local trends and allows them to supply customers with the fashions they want.

Adapted from: Article in The Economist 18/06/05

(*a*) Describe the **advantages** and **disadvantages** of using a "just-in-time" approach. — KU 4

(*b*) Describe **2** methods of Vertical Integration. Give **one** advantage of **each** method. — KU 4

(*c*) Suggest and justify **2** ways in which ICT can be used to **communicate information to customers**. — DM 4

(*d*) Suggest and describe **2** ways in which Zara can **gather information** to give customers fashions they want. — DM 4

DO NOT WRITE IN THIS MARGIN

	KU	DM

2.

"The Unique Motor Company has a simple philosophy in that we aim to provide innovative, practical vehicles that are both safe and reliable and yet fun and affordable"

Noel Edmonds, Chairman

The Qpod range was launched in the UK in June 2004 by the Unique Motor Company(UK). The Qpod City is classed as a moped that can be driven by 16 year olds. Unlike quad bikes, which cannot legally be driven on a public road, the Qpod can be driven both on and off road.

Market Research has shown that there is a need for a versatile vehicle which can be used almost anywhere. The Unique Motor Company are planning to market the product to as wide a range of consumers as possible from young teenagers to the elderly and disabled people. Some police forces in the UK are using them successfully in and out of town.

Source: www.uniquemotorcompany.co.uk

(*a*) Describe the steps which are taken by a business **before a product is launched**. **4** (KU)

(*b*) (i) Identify **which stage of the Product Life Cycle** the Qpod was at in June 2004. Describe what happens at this stage. **3** (DM)

(ii) Name and describe the **next 3 stages** a product will go through in its life cycle. **6** (KU)

[Turn over

DO NOT WRITE IN THIS MARGIN

KU DM

3. Anita Sadiq started her mobile hairdressing service a year ago. She has now prepared her final accounts for the first year and is quite pleased with the results.

Here is Anita's Trading, Profit & Loss Account:

Hair at Home
Trading, Profit & Loss Account
for the period ended 31 March 2006

	£	£
Sales		35,000
Less: Cost of Sales		
Opening Stock	6,200	
Add: Purchases	12,300	
	18,500	
Less: Closing Stock	4,200	
		14,300
GROSS PROFIT		20,700
Less: Expenses		
Telephone Calls	1,200	
Petrol	1,600	
Advertising	1,000	
Miscellaneous	500	
		4,300
NET PROFIT		16,400

(*a*) (i) Identify **2 profitability ratios** that Anita could use to analyse her Trading, Profit & Loss Account. 2

(ii) Using the figures from Anita's Trading, Profit & Loss Account, **calculate one of the ratios** you have identified above. 3

(*b*) Anita is thinking of recruiting an employee to assist her.

Describe **steps in the recruitment process** that Anita should take to do this. 4

(*c*) Give **one** example of a **piece of employment legislation** and state the affect it would have on Anita's business. 2

DO NOT WRITE IN THIS MARGIN

KU DM

4.

High street sales fell for a record sixth consecutive month in August 2005. The gloom in the Business Cycle comes as another survey suggests that firms are being hit by a slowdown in the economy.

Other external factors have been affecting retailers. Shops have been forced to continue sales into the autumn season. Lowering prices to gain customers is reducing profit margins. Prices cannot get much lower or some of the most famous names on the UK high street will fail.

Adapted from: The Scotsman 05-09-2005 & 06-09-2005

(*a*) Identify and describe **2** stages of the **Business Cycle**. KU 4

(*b*) (i) Other than "a slowdown in the economy" identify and describe **2** **external factors** that could affect high street retailers. KU 4

(ii) What **effect** could external factors **have on decisions** made by managers in a high street store? DM 2

(*c*) Other than lowering prices, what decisions can high street shops make to **avoid failure**? DM 4

[Turn over for Question 5 on *Page six*

5. THE LOCHS HOTEL
ISLE OF LEWIS

The Lochs Hotel is a luxury hotel in the Highlands of Scotland. The owners of the hotel are considering a restructuring programme by removing the supervisors level. At present the staff are organised as follows:

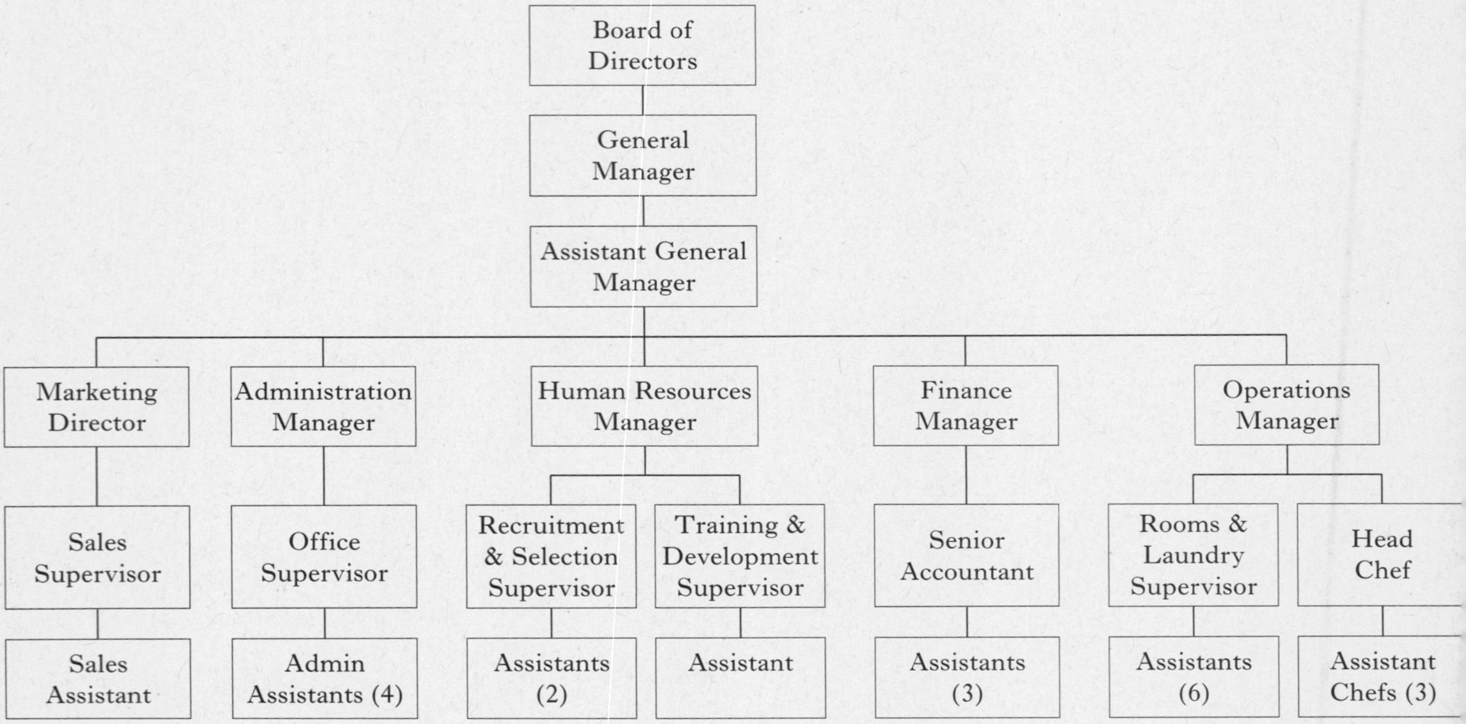

DO NOT WRITE IN THIS MARGIN

		KU	DM
(*a*)	(i) Explain the term **functional relationship**.	2	
	(ii) Give **2** examples from the chart above.		2
(*b*)	(i) Name the proposed type of **restructuring** of the hotel.	1	
	(ii) Describe the **possible effects** of this on the hotel.		3
(*c*)	Identify **4** possible **aims** this hotel could have.		4
(*d*)	Suggest and justify **2 ways** in which managers can **develop employees** to ensure the hotel achieves its aims.		4

[*END OF QUESTION PAPER*]

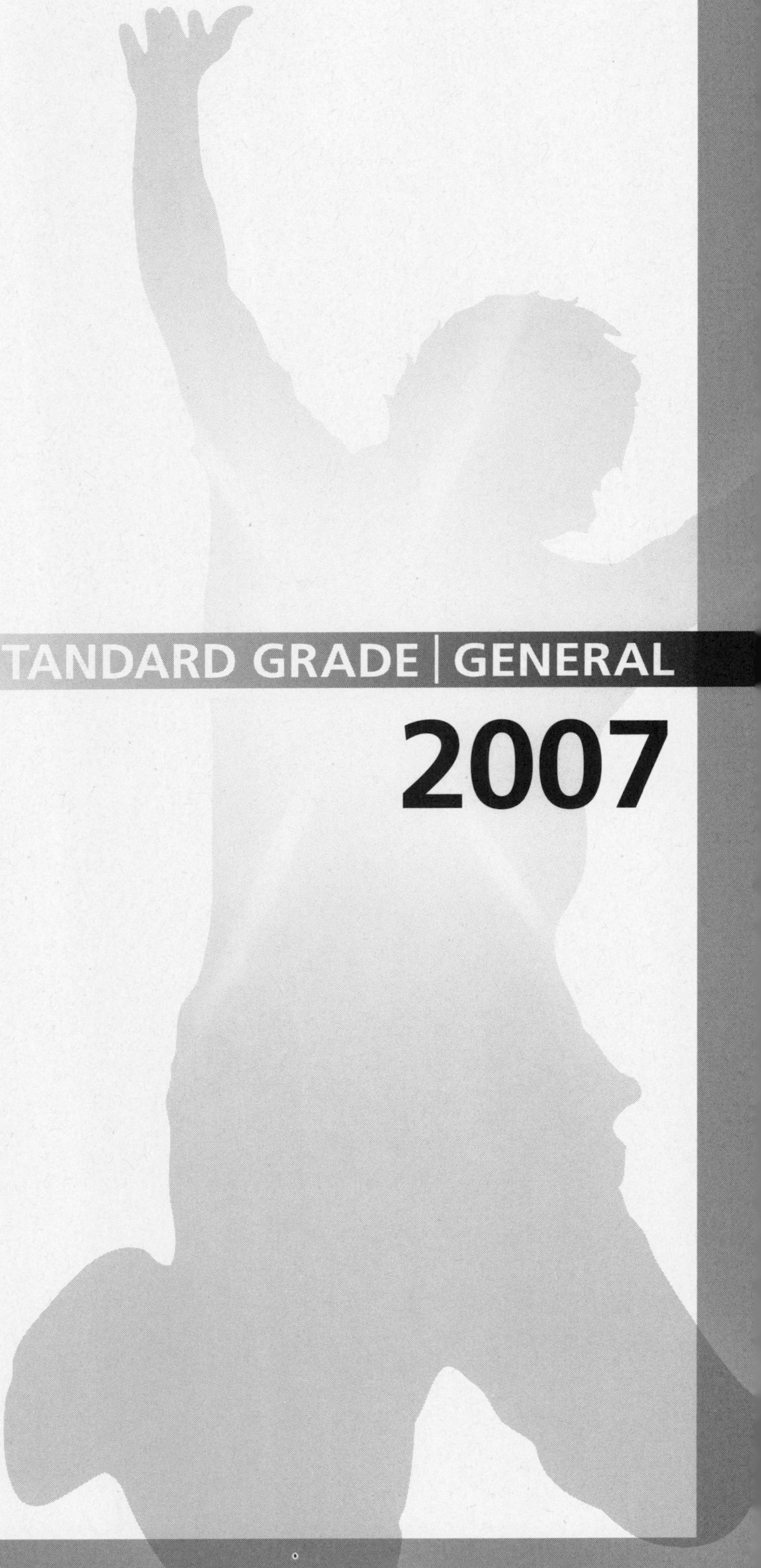

STANDARD GRADE | GENERAL

2007

[BLANK PAGE]

FOR OFFICIAL USE

G

	KU	DM
Total		

4200/402

NATIONAL QUALIFICATIONS 2007

MONDAY, 14 MAY
10.20 AM – 11.35 AM

BUSINESS MANAGEMENT
STANDARD GRADE
General Level

Fill in these boxes and read what is printed below.

Full name of centre

Town

Forename(s)

Surname

Date of birth
Day Month Year

Scottish candidate number

Number of seat

1 Read each question carefully.

2 Attempt **all** the questions.

3 All answers are to be written in this answer book.

4 Do **not** write in the margins.

5 Before leaving the examination room you must give this book to the invigilator. If you do not, you may lose all the marks for this paper.

LI 4200/402 6/12570

DO NOT WRITE IN THIS MARGIN

Marks KU DM

1. Study the information below and then answer the questions that follow.

> **GREGGS**
>
> Greggs plc has as one of its aims to be Europe's finest bakery by providing quality goods and services to customers. Their purpose is "the growth of our business for the benefit and enjoyment of all our stakeholders".
>
> People are very important to them and whenever possible recruitment for promoted posts is done internally.
>
> **Adapted from Greggs website**

(*a*) Explain the terms:

goods ______________________________

____

services ______________________________

______________________________ 2

(*b*) Suggest and justify **2** ways in which Greggs plc could grow in size. Give 2 **different** justifications.

Suggestion 1 ______________________________

Justification ______________________________

____

Suggestion 2 ______________________________

Justification ______________________________

______________________________ 4

(*c*) Give **2** reasons why Greggs plc may **want** to grow in size.

1 ______________________________

____

2 ______________________________

______________________________ 2

DO NOT WRITE IN THIS MARGIN

Marks KU DM

1. (continued)

(*d*) Identify **3** possible **stakeholders** in Greggs plc.

1 ____________________

2 ____________________

3 ____________________ **3**

(*e*) Give **2** possible **reasons** why Greggs plc may prefer to recruit internally.

1 ____________________

____

2 ____________________

____________________ **2**

(*f*) (i) Suggest **one** method Greggs plc could use to recruit externally.

____

____________________ **1**

(ii) Give **one advantage** and **one disadvantage** of this method of recruitment.

Advantage ____________________

____

Disadvantage ____________________

____________________ **2**

[Turn over

DO NOT WRITE IN THIS MARGIN

Marks | KU | DM

2. Study the information below and then answer the questions that follow.

Malik Co Ltd manufactures toy cars. Below is a table showing its fixed costs and variable costs of production.

COSTS OF PRODUCTION		
Output	**Fixed Costs**	**Variable Costs**
1000	10,000	30,000
2000	10,000	45,000
3000	10,000	60,000
4000	10,000	70,000

(*a*) Explain the terms:

(i) Fixed Costs ______________________________

____

(ii) Variable Costs ______________________________

______________________________ **2**

(*b*) Give an example for Malik Co Ltd of:

(i) A Fixed Cost ______________________________

(ii) A Variable Cost ______________________________ **2**

(*c*) What **sector of industry** does Malik Co Ltd operate in?

______________________________ **1**

(*d*) Name **one other** sector of industry.

______________________________ **1**

[Turn over for Question 3 on *Page six*

DO NOT WRITE IN THIS MARGIN

Marks KU DM

3. Study the information below and then answer the questions that follow.

Island Bakery Organics is a small family run business on the Isle of Mull. The business makes a range of organic biscuits using as little mechanisation as possible and then distributes them across the country. They are planning a number of new product launches over the next 12 months using television advertising and in-store sampling of their products.

They are also designing new packaging for their products as they feel this is important in attracting customers.

Adapted from www.islandbakery.co.uk

(*a*) Explain the term **mechanisation**.

____

____ **1**

(*b*) Suggest **2 reasons** why the business uses as little mechanisation as possible in their production process.

Reason 1 ______________________________________

____

Reason 2 ______________________________________

____ **2**

DO NOT WRITE IN THIS MARGIN

Marks | KU | DM

3. (continued)

(*c*) Other than using new packaging, suggest and justify **2 ways** in which new customers could be attracted. Give 2 **different** justifications.

Suggestion 1 ______________________________

Justification ______________________________

____

Suggestion 2 ______________________________

Justification ______________________________

______________________________ **4**

(*d*) Identify a suitable **channel of distribution** which Island Bakery Organics could use to get their products to customers.

____

______________________________ **1**

(*e*) Suggest **2 possible reasons** why Island Bakery Organics may have decided to locate on the Isle of Mull.

1 ______________________________

____

2 ______________________________

______________________________ **2**

[Turn over

DO NOT WRITE IN THIS MARGIN

Marks | KU | DM

4. Study the information below and then answer the questions that follow.

Robbie Williams owns one, Posh and Becks have his 'n her models—the iPOD!

An innovation from Apple is the iPOD nano which, as well as letting you download up to 10,000 songs from the Internet, is now as thin as a pencil.

(*a*) Explain the term **innovation**.

____

________________________________ **1**

(*b*) Suggest and justify **one market segment** which Apple may be targeting with the iPOD nano.

Market Segment ________________________

____

Justification ________________________

________________________________ **2**

(*c*) Identify **2 external influences** which could affect sales of the iPOD nano.

1 ______________________________

____

2 ______________________________

________________________________ **2**

DO NOT WRITE IN THIS MARGIN

Marks | KU | DM

4. (continued)

(*d*) Suggest and justify **2 methods of communication** which Apple **employees** could use world wide. Give 2 **different** justifications.

Method 1 ________________________________

Justification ________________________________

____

Method 2 ________________________________

Justification ________________________________

________________________________ 4

(*e*) Apple uses television advertising. Suggest **2 reasons** why they use this form of advertising.

1 ________________________________

____

2 ________________________________

________________________________ 2

[Turn over

DO NOT WRITE IN THIS MARGIN

Marks | KU | DM

5. Study the information below and then answer the questions that follow.

LOCH FYNE

Loch Fyne Oysters started out as a small oyster farm and has now grown to be the largest producer of oysters in the UK. The company has grown to include a smokehouse, an oyster bar, restaurant and shop. Ordering can now be done on-line. Further diversification is planned.

Relief of poverty, providing education and protection of the environment are also very important at Loch Fyne Oysters.

Adapted from www.lochfyne.com

(*a*) Explain the term **diversification**.

____

____ **1**

(*b*) Suggest **2** reasons why Loch Fyne Oysters may have decided to diversify.

1 ____

____

2 ____

____ **2**

(*c*) Suggest **2 advantages** to Loch Fyne Oysters of allowing customers to order on-line.

1 ____

____

2 ____

____ **2**

DO NOT WRITE IN THIS MARGIN

Marks KU DM

5. (continued)

(*d*) Give **one benefit** to Loch Fyne Oysters of being involved in protecting the environment.

____

____ 1

(*e*) Suggest **2 ways** in which Loch Fyne Oysters can help protect the environment.

1 ____

____

____

2 ____

____

____ 2

[Turn over

DO NOT WRITE IN THIS MARGIN

Marks | KU | DM

6. Study the information below and then answer the questions that follow.

Gordon Deuchars started G.A. Engineering with the support of The Prince's Trust and it is now one of the leading engineering companies working in the North of Scotland.

People are important to Gordon. He values the opinions of all employees and consults with them in making decisions. All recruitment procedures are followed and every employee receives a contract of employment.

Prince's Trust

Adapted from Prince's Trust website

(*a*) Suggest **2** ways in which The Prince's Trust may have helped Gordon Deuchars start his business.

1 ______________________________

____

____

2 ______________________________

____

______________________________ **2**

(*b*) Identify the **style of management** being used at G.A. Engineering.

______________________________ **1**

(*c*) Name and describe **another** style of management.

Style of management ______________________________

Description ______________________________

____

______________________________ **2**

DO NOT WRITE IN THIS MARGIN

Marks KU DM

6. (continued)

(*d*) Apart from your Job Title, name **2** items which would appear on a Contract of Employment.

1 ____

____

2 ____

____ **2**

(*e*) When recruiting staff, G.A. Engineering prepares a Job Description. Identify **2 pieces of information** contained in a Job Description.

1 ____

____

2 ____

____ **2**

[*END OF QUESTION PAPER*]

[BLANK PAGE]

STANDARD GRADE | CREDIT

2007

[BLANK PAGE]

C

4200/403

NATIONAL QUALIFICATIONS 2007

MONDAY, 14 MAY
1.00 PM – 2.30 PM

BUSINESS MANAGEMENT
STANDARD GRADE
Credit Level

1 Read each question carefully.

2 Attempt **all** the questions.

3 All answers are to be written in the answer book provided.

LI 4200/403 6/7470

DO NOT WRITE IN THIS MARGIN

KU | DM

1.

MACKIE'S
of Scotland

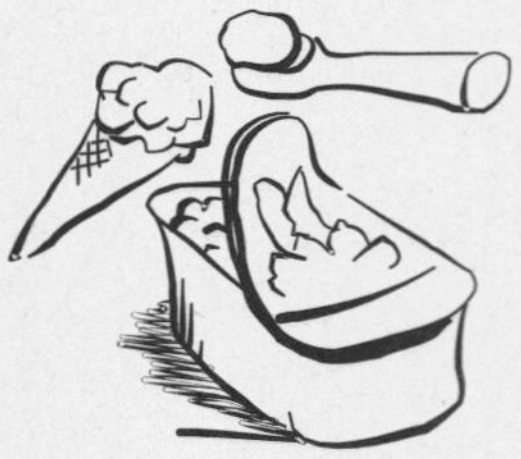

Mackie's has 11% of the premium ice-cream market in the UK and is the brand leader in Scotland.

Mackie's has over 500 cows—the largest Jersey herd in the UK. Jerseys are used to meet Mackie's "designer milk" requirement—because Jerseys produce the creamiest milk. The process from milking to ice-cream can be completed in under 24 hours. £600,000 has been invested in robotic milking and 9 milking robots have been installed.

Since its popularity in the 2002 Seoul Olympics—Mackie's of Asia has plans to increase from its current base of 35 branded ice-cream/cafe parlours to 200 franchises in South Korea. From there it intends to expand throughout Asia with early plans to investigate Japan. Organic produce is popular in Korea and consumer tests in Korea show similar excitement about a new fresh and natural ice cream from Scotland.

Adapted from: www.mackies.co.uk

(*a*) Name and describe the **method of production** which Mackie's uses to manufacture ice-cream. Give **2 problems** of using this method. **4** (KU)

(*b*) Explain the importance to the company of having a **strong brand**. **2** (KU)

(*c*) Give **2 reasons** why Mackie's has **invested in robotic milking equipment** for its factory. **2** (KU)

(*d*) Suggest and describe a suitable **pricing strategy** that Mackie's could use for its ice-cream. Justify your choice. **3** (DM)

(*e*) Other than price, suggest and justify **3 appropriate marketing strategies** that Mackie's could use when expanding its market to Japan. **6** (DM)

DO NOT WRITE IN THIS MARGIN

KU DM

2.

amazon.com©

Amazon.com is one of the biggest "E-Commerce" businesses in the world. Amazon.com sells a wide variety of goods and services on-line. Amazon's UK distribution centre is a large warehouse for storing stock. However, you won't see space age robots picking goods off shelves. Labour intensive processing is used, with hands stuffing books into pigeon holes, stacking CDs onto shelves and moving electrical appliances around the warehouse floor.

A huge banner above the workers' heads reads ***"Safety protects people. Quality protects customers"***.

Adapted from: "The Internet" Magazine, September 2003

(*a*) Describe the **features of a suitable stock storage area** for Amazon. 3

(*b*) Suggest and describe **a suitable computerised stock control system** that Amazon may use to keep track of its products. 2

(*c*) Describe the **advantages** and **disadvantages** to be gained from operating as an "E-Commerce" business. 4

(*d*) Suggest reasons why Amazon uses **labour intensive** processes in the distribution centre. 2

(*e*) Suggest ways in which Amazon can ensure:

(i) safety of its employees in the warehouse; 3

(ii) a quality service to its customers. 3

[Turn over

DO NOT WRITE IN THIS MARGIN

KU | DM

3. Fredo Franchi's fast food business has been running for one year now and he has plans to expand by opening another shop. His brother Carlo is considering joining him in partnership and wants to look at the business finances. Fredo has prepared a Cash Budget for him to look at before making a decision.

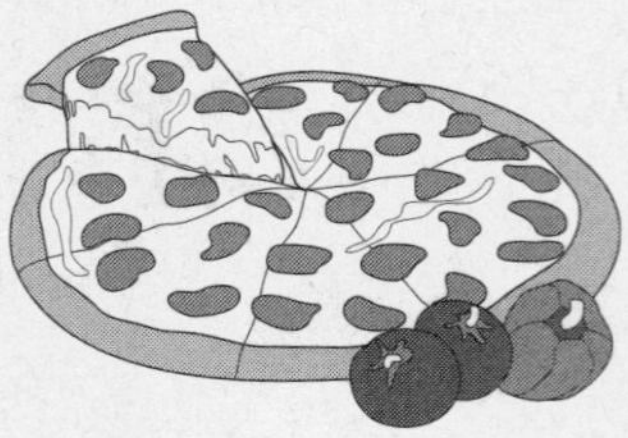

CASH BUDGET—FRANCHI FAST FOODS **JUNE–AUGUST 2007**			
	June	**July**	**August**
Opening Balance	£500	£2,300	–£1,000
Cash In			
Sales	£27,500	£30,000	£33,000
	£28,000	£32,300	£32,000
Cash Out			
Purchases	£10,600	£15,000	£13,000
Wages	£9,600	£10,500	£11,500
Expenses	£5,500	£7,800	£9,800
	£25,700	£33,300	£34,300
Closing Balance	£2,300	–£1,000	–£2,300

(*a*) Explain the **purpose** of preparing a Cash Budget. **2** (KU)

(*b*) (i) Give **3** reasons why Carlo might be concerned about the cashflow situation. **3** (DM)

(ii) Suggest **appropriate action** that can be taken to improve the **3** problems you have identified above. **3** (DM)

(*c*) (i) Identify **2 potential problems** that Fredo and Carlo might have in forming a partnership. **2** (KU)

(ii) Suggest **2 different ways** in which they can overcome these problems. **2** (DM)

(*d*) What **factors** should Fredo consider before deciding where to locate his new shop? **2** (KU)

DO NOT WRITE IN THIS MARGIN

KU DM

4.

PENNY-SAVE LTD

Saves-mart Stores and Pennyways supermarkets are two leading low-cost supermarkets in the UK. They have recently merged and have become "Penny-Save Ltd". As a result of the merger the business underwent a massive restructuring process.

The business has de-layered its workforce with the loss of thousands of jobs. Penny-Save Ltd now has a flat structure, which is designed to make the business more competitive and efficient. One of the main benefits to be gained from the merger will be greater economies of scale.

Although the restructuring process will eventually save the business money, the merger has increased costs and profits are likely to fall this year. In addition, 2 major German low-cost supermarkets have announced plans to merge—this will make **them** the new market leader.

(*a*) Explain how changing to a **flat structure** can make Penny-Save Ltd **more efficient**. 2

(*b*) Describe **2 economies of scale** that Penny-Save Ltd can benefit from after merging. 2

(*c*) Identify steps in a **decision making model** that Penny-Save Ltd could use to face competition from the new market leader. 4

(*d*) Suggest and justify **2 ways** in which Penny-Save Ltd **can compete** with the new market leader. 4

[Turn over for Question 5 on *Page six*

DO NOT WRITE IN THIS MARGIN

KU DM

5.

Traditional Goodness

About 330 jobs were lost with the closure of the Grampian Country Foods factory in Buckie, Aberdeenshire. The company said a £16m redevelopment of its site at Broxburn near Edinburgh would create 200 jobs.

The management consulted with employees in an effort to avoid redundancy. This included securing alternative employment either within the business or with other local firms. These measures were taken to avoid potential industrial action from the employees.

Source: www.scotsman.com

(*a*) Describe the **possible effects** of the factory closure on the local economy. 2

(*b*) Suggest and justify **2 ways** in which the management could "**consult with employees**" to avoid redundancies. 4

(*c*) Name and describe **2 forms of Industrial Action** which employees could take. 4

[*END OF QUESTION PAPER*]

STANDARD GRADE | GENERAL

2008

[BLANK PAGE]

FOR OFFICIAL USE

G

	KU	DM
Total		

4200/402

NATIONAL QUALIFICATIONS 2008

FRIDAY, 16 MAY
10.20 AM – 11.35 AM

BUSINESS MANAGEMENT
STANDARD GRADE
General Level

Fill in these boxes and read what is printed below.

Full name of centre

Town

Forename(s)

Surname

Date of birth
Day Month Year

Scottish candidate number

Number of seat

1 Read each question carefully.

2 Attempt **all** the questions.

3 All answers are to be written in this answer book.

4 Do **not** write in the margins.

5 Before leaving the examination room you must give this book to the invigilator. If you do not, you may lose all the marks for this paper.

DO NOT WRITE IN THIS MARGIN

Marks KU DM

1. Study the information below and then answer the questions that follow.

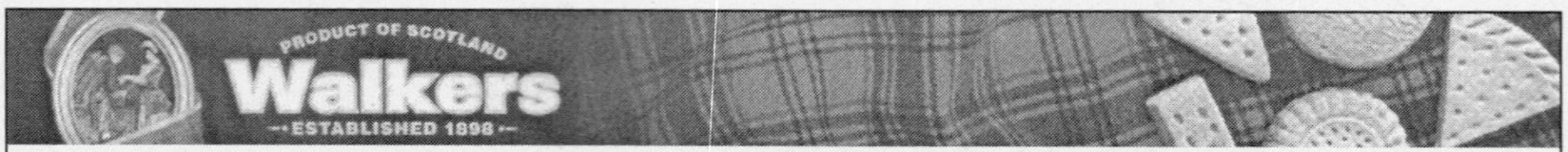

Walkers Shortbread Ltd of Speyside is one of Scotland's leading manufacturers of shortbread. The company has introduced the latest computerised technology in the production process. Walkers Shortbread Ltd, however, still bakes its products in small batches to keep the traditional flavour and appearance for which it is famous.

Adapted from Walkers Shortbread Ltd website

(*a*) Identify the type of business organisation run by Walkers.

______________________________ **1**

(*b*) Suggest **2** suitable aims of Walkers Shortbread Ltd.

1 ______________________________

____

2 ______________________________

______________________________ **2**

(*c*) Suggest and justify **2** different places where Walkers Shortbread Ltd could sell its products. **Use a different justification for each suggestion.**

Suggestion 1 ______________________________

Justification ______________________________

____

Suggestion 2 ______________________________

Justification ______________________________

______________________________ **4**

DO NOT WRITE IN THIS MARGIN

Marks KU DM

1. (continued)

(*d*) Walkers Shortbread Ltd uses batch production. Identify **one advantage** and **one disadvantage** of using this method of production.

Advantage ______________________________

____

Disadvantage ______________________________

______________________________ **2**

(*e*) Identify and describe **2** other methods of production.

Method of Production ______________________________

Description ______________________________

____

Method of Production ______________________________

Description ______________________________

______________________________ **4**

(*f*) State **one benefit** to Walkers Shortbread Ltd of using computerised technology in the production process.

____

______________________________ **1**

(*g*) Suggest a problem **to the workforce** of the introduction of computerised technology.

____

______________________________ **1**

[Turn over

DO NOT WRITE IN THIS MARGIN

Marks | KU | DM

2. Below are the mobile phone sales figures for Teckno Sales Ltd for the 3 months January – March.

	A	B	C	D	E
1	SALESPERSON	JANUARY	FEBRUARY	MARCH	SALES PERSON TOTAL
2	T Asif	£800	£750	£850	£2,400
3	S Meechan	£120	£120	£120	£360
4	J Kourimska	£500	£450	£500	£1,450
5	TOTAL SALES	£1,420	£1,320	£1,470	£4,210

(*a*) Name the piece of **software** used to create the information shown above.

______________________________ **1**

(*b*) From the information shown above, identify the salesperson who has the **highest** total sales.

______________________________ **1**

(*c*) From the information shown above, identify the month with the **lowest** total sales.

______________________________ **1**

(*d*) Suggest **one** reason why the Sales Manager is concerned about the sales figures from S Meechan.

____

______________________________ **1**

DO NOT WRITE IN THIS MARGIN

	Marks	KU	DM
2. (continued)			
(*e*) Suggest and justify **2** promotional methods which could be used by Teckno Sales Ltd. **Use a different justification for each suggestion.** Suggestion 1 ______ Justification ______ Suggestion 2 ______ Justification ______	4		
(*f*) Teckno Sales Ltd needs to find out what its customers want. Suggest a type of market research which it could use. Give **one advantage** and **one disadvantage** of this type of market research. Method ______	1		
Advantage ______ Disadvantage ______	2		

[Turn over

DO NOT WRITE IN THIS MARGIN

Marks | KU | DM

3. Balance Sheet of Gillespie Manufacturing Ltd as at 31 December 2007

	£000	£000
<u>Fixed Assets</u>		
Premises		300
Vehicles		100
		400
<u>Current Assets</u>		
Stock	20	
Debtors	50	
Cash	15	
	85	
<u>Current Liabilities</u>		
Creditors	65	
Working Capital		20
		£420
<u>Financed by</u>		
Capital		390
Net Profit		30
		£420

(*a*) Explain the terms:

Fixed Assets ____

Current Assets ____

Current Liabilities ____ **3**

DO NOT WRITE IN THIS MARGIN

	Marks	KU	DM
3. (continued)			
(*b*) (i) State the formula for calculating Working Capital (Current) ratio.	2		
(ii) If the Working Capital ratio was too low, suggest **one** way in which it could be improved.	1		
(*c*) Other than the Balance Sheet, state the final account the net profit will appear in.	1		

[Turn over

DO NOT WRITE IN THIS MARGIN

Marks KU DM

4. Rooney Bus Company Limited operates a flat organisation structure.

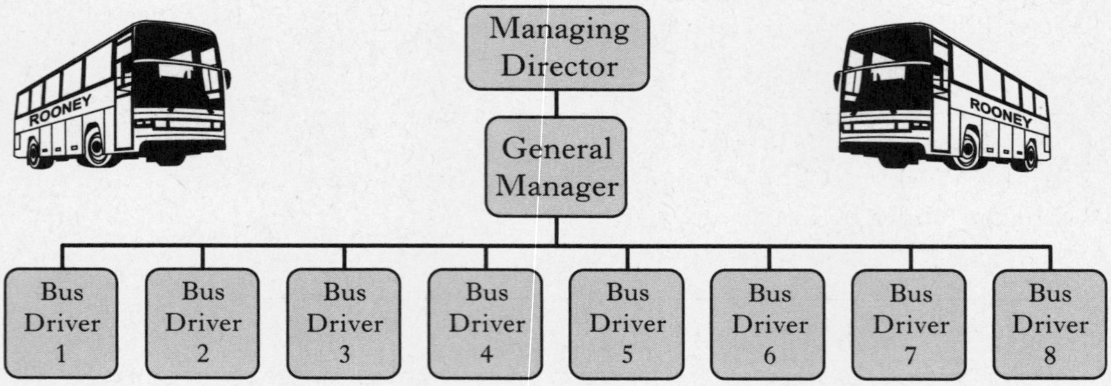

(*a*) State **2** advantages of a flat organisaton structure.

1 ____

2 ____ **2**

(*b*) Identify and describe **another** type of organisation structure.

Organisation Structure ______________________________

Description ______________________________________

____

____ **2**

(*c*) From the organisation chart above, give an example of a line relationship.

____

____ **1**

(*d*) Describe the term **chain of command**.

____

____

____ **1**

[Turn over for Question 5 on *Page ten*

DO NOT WRITE IN THIS MARGIN

Marks KU DM

5. Study the information below and then answer the questions that follow.

> Spar is a food chain which operates in a national and multi-national market. It has over 900 different products in its own brand range with 75% of customers preferring to buy Spar brands. Spar recognises the importance of getting the best employees. Recruitment is done both internally and externally. Spar aims to be a good employer.
>
> SPAR
>
> **Adapted from Spar Website**

(*a*) Explain the term **multi-national market**.

____

________________________________ **1**

(*b*) State **one** advantage to Spar of having "own brand" labels.

____

________________________________ **1**

(*c*) Suggest **2** ways that "own brands" can compete with well known brands.

1 ________________________________

____

2 ________________________________

________________________________ **2**

(*d*) Explain the terms "internal" and "external" recruitment.

Internal ________________________________

____

External ________________________________

________________________________ **2**

DO NOT WRITE IN THIS MARGIN

Marks KU DM

5. (continued)

(*e*) Suggest **one** way that Spar could recruit externally.

____

____ **1**

(*f*) Suggest a selection process, other than by interview, which Spar could use to recruit staff.

____

____ **1**

(*g*) Suggest **2** ways Spar could be a good employer.

1 ____

____

2 ____

____ **2**

[Turn over

DO NOT WRITE IN THIS MARGIN

Marks KU DM

6. Study the information below and then answer the questions that follow.

> Dobbies plc has a large number of garden centres in the UK, providing a wide range of gardening and home products. Many customers pay £10 a year to join its gardening club and benefit by receiving discounts and offers. Communication with its customers is important and this is done through its website as well as in the garden centre.
>
> **Adapted from Dobbies website: www.dobbies.com**

(*a*) Give **one** advantage and **one** disadvantage to Dobbies plc of being a public limited company.

Advantage ______________________________

____

Disadvantage ______________________________

______________________________ **2**

(*b*) Suggest **one** benefit to Dobbies plc of having a gardening club scheme.

____

______________________________ **1**

(*c*) Other than contact details, identify **2** pieces of information which Dobbies plc might have on its website.

1 ______________________________

____

2 ______________________________

______________________________ **2**

DO NOT WRITE IN THIS MARGIN

Marks KU DM

6. (continued)

(*d*) Suggest **3** ways of making the website more attractive.

1 ______________________________________

2 ______________________________________

3 ______________________________________ **3**

(*e*) Dobbies plc uses both formal and informal communication. Study the pictures below then answer the questions that follow.

Picture 1

Picture 2

(i) Identify whether the above pictures are showing a method of formal or informal communication. Insert the word "formal" or "informal" against the picture number below.

Picture 1 ______________________________________

Picture 2 ______________________________________ **2**

(ii) Suggest **one** benefit of picture 2 as a method of communication.

____

______________________________________ **1**

[*END OF QUESTION PAPER*]

[BLANK PAGE]

STANDARD GRADE | CREDIT

2008

[BLANK PAGE]

C

4200/403

NATIONAL QUALIFICATIONS 2008

FRIDAY, 16 MAY
1.00 PM – 2.30 PM

BUSINESS MANAGEMENT
STANDARD GRADE
Credit Level

1 Read each question carefully.

2 Attempt **all** the questions.

3 All answers are to be written in the answer book provided.

DO NOT WRITE IN THIS MARGIN

KU DM

1.

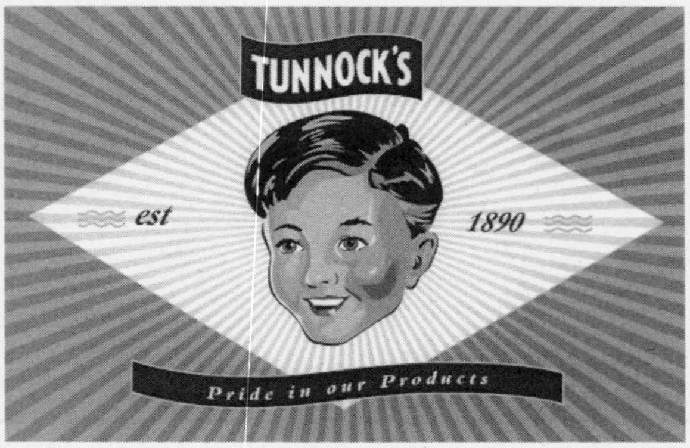

"TUNNOCK'S TASTEFUL PAST . . .
Thomas Tunnock started Thomas Tunnock Ltd in Uddingston in 1890. The management has always remained true to the original principles of producing high quality products."

"EATING INTO WORLD MARKETS . . .
Tunnock's biscuits are more than just a Scottish phenomenon. They are in demand around the world—as far apart as the Caribbean, Kuwait, Japan and Canada. Tunnock's future aim is to convert even more countries to these Scottish delights."

Adapted from: www.tunnock.co.uk

(*a*) Describe ways in which Tunnock's can ensure it produces a high quality product. 4

(*b*) (i) Describe the role of a Manager. 4

(ii) Outline details that could be included in a Job Description for a **Production** Manager in Tunnock's. 4

(*c*) Suggest reasons why Tunnock's wants to expand its global market. 2

DO NOT WRITE IN THIS MARGIN

KU | DM

2.

HOUSE OF FRASER

House of Fraser has taken over Jenners—the oldest independent department store in the world. It has maintained its original position at 48 Princes Street, Edinburgh, since 1838. Jenners sells a wide range of luxury goods from quality furniture to designer clothes. House of Fraser has agreed to keep the "Jenners" brand name on its shops.

The Board of House of Fraser believes that the take-over will generate economies of scale. The addition of the Jenners brand will strengthen the reputation of the business as the UK's leading retailer of designer goods.

Source: Adapted from House of Fraser Website: Press Release – 21-03-05

(*a*) (i) Explain the term **economies of scale**. Give **2 examples** of internal economies of scale that House of Fraser will gain from this take-over. — KU **3**

(ii) Other than economies of scale, give **one advantage** and **one disadvantage** of a take-over. — KU **2**

(*b*) Identify **3 advantages** to be gained from having a strong brand. — KU **3**

(*c*) (i) Identify a market segment most likely to purchase luxury goods. — DM **1**

(ii) Suggest and justify **2** appropriate places to advertise the stores to attract the attention of this market segment. — DM **4**

[Turn over

DO NOT WRITE IN THIS MARGIN

KU DM

3.

Thomson Holidays' call centre was set up at Cardonald Business Park in 1999 with help from Scottish Enterprise. It received a government grant—Regional Selective Assistance worth £1·4 m when it opened.

In December 2006 Thomson closed its Glasgow call centre with the loss of 450 jobs. More people are now choosing to book on-line rather than by phone. Since the centre opened in 1999, the company's Internet bookings had increased from 10% to 50%.

Source: adapted from article www.bbc.co.uk/news 30-08-2006

(*a*) Suggest reasons why the Government may award Regional Selective Assistance. **2** (KU)

(*b*) Other than selling holidays, suggest and justify **3 reasons** why Thomson uses the Internet. **6** (DM)

(*c*) (i) Identify **2 stakeholders** other than employees that will be affected by the closure of the call centre. Describe their interest in the business. **4** (DM)

(ii) Explain how the interests of employees might conflict with other stakeholders in the business. **2** (DM)

DO NOT WRITE IN THIS MARGIN

	KU	DM

4.

FINANCE

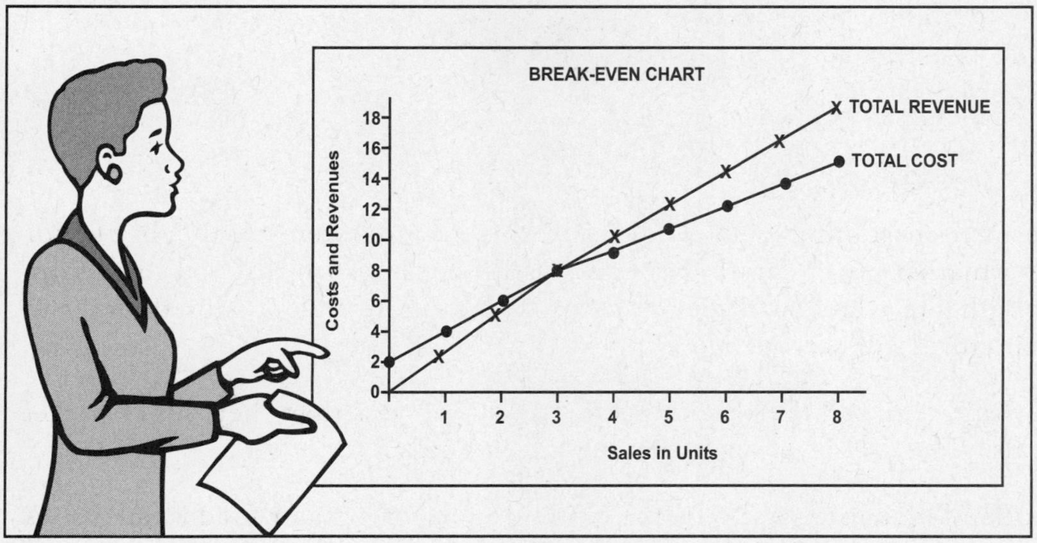

Martina Fernandez wants to set up a greetings card business. She is preparing her Business Plan but is concerned about her costs—she will need to work very hard just to break-even.

(*a*) Explain the purpose of a Business Plan. **KU: 2**

(*b*) Describe the following terms and give examples of each.

(i) Fixed costs **KU: 2**

(ii) Variable costs **KU: 2**

(*c*) Explain the term "break-even". **KU: 2**

(*d*) Describe **3 risks** involved in starting a business. **KU: 3**

(*e*) Describe and justify **2 decisions** that Martina will need to make when planning her business. **DM: 4**

[Turn over for Question 5 on *Page six*

DO NOT WRITE IN THIS MARGIN

	KU	DM

5.

German discount chains Lidl and Aldi are to intensify the battle for supermarket customers in Scotland. Aldi has a £20 m distribution centre in Bathgate which will enable them to distribute their goods directly to their stores in Scotland more quickly.

Lidl and Aldi sell their products for about 30% less than their supermarket rivals. They achieve this by having lower costs.

Scotland is shaping up to be the battleground for a major food retail war as a number of supermarket giants square up to each other with expansion plans. The 2 biggest UK supermarket chains—Tesco and Asda can't ignore these discount rivals for much longer.

Source: adapted from an article in Scotland on Sunday – 06-08-2006

(*a*) State **one advantage** and **one disadvantage** of distributing directly to shops. 2

(*b*) Describe ways in which Lidl and Aldi could achieve lower costs than rivals. 4

(*c*) Describe possible costs and benefits to the local economy of supermarket expansion. 4

(*d*) Suggest reasons why customers might still prefer to shop in Tesco or Asda. 4

[*END OF QUESTION PAPER*]

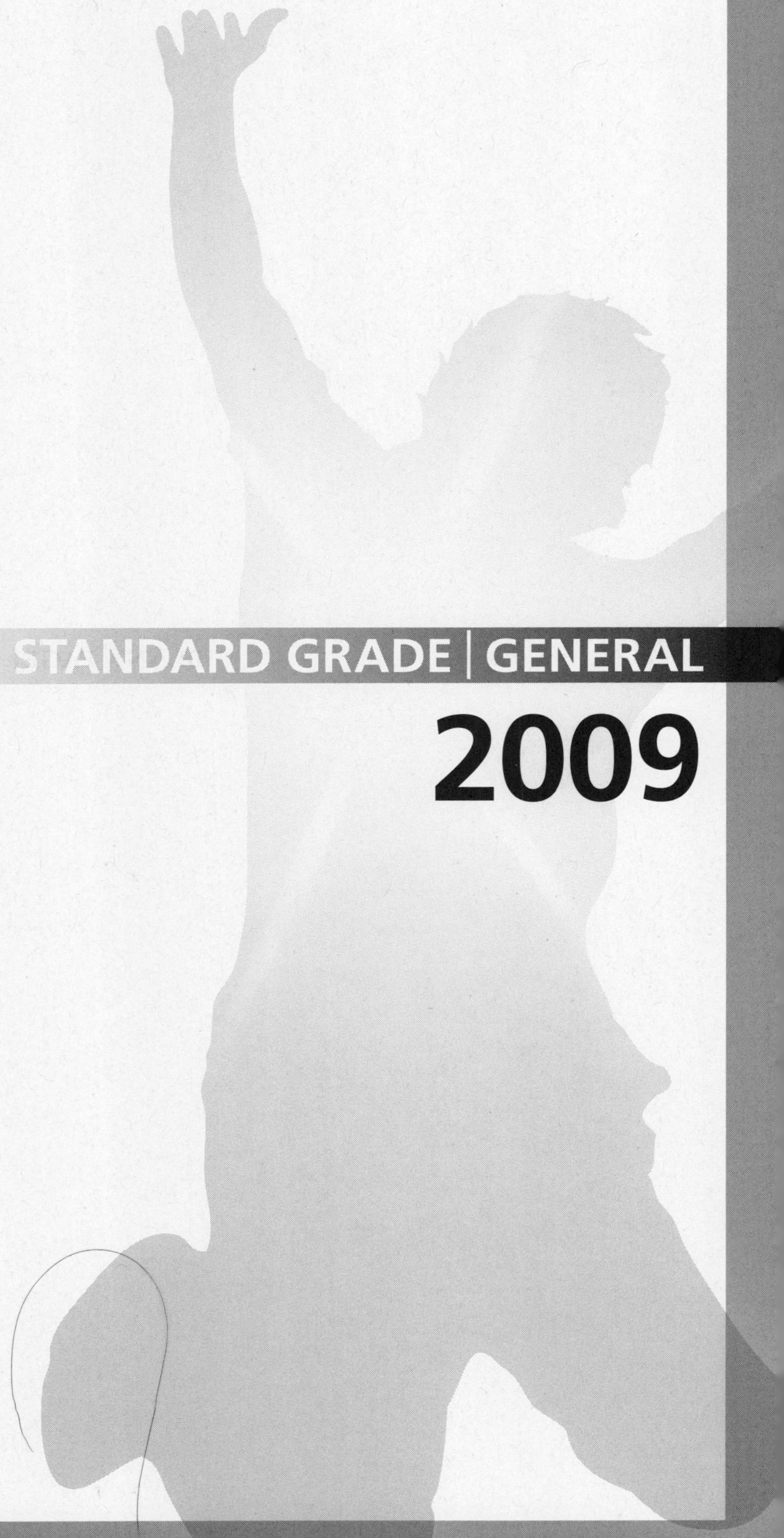

STANDARD GRADE | GENERAL

2009

[BLANK PAGE]

FOR OFFICIAL USE

G

	KU	DM
Total		

4200/402

NATIONAL QUALIFICATIONS 2009

TUESDAY, 19 MAY
10.20 AM – 11.35 AM

BUSINESS MANAGEMENT
STANDARD GRADE
General Level

Fill in these boxes and read what is printed below.

Full name of centre

Town

Forename(s)

Surname

Date of birth
Day Month Year

Scottish candidate number

Number of seat

1 Read each question carefully.

2 Attempt **all** the questions.

3 All answers are to be written in this answer book.

4 Do **not** write in the margins.

5 Before leaving the examination room you must give this book to the invigilator. If you do not, you may lose all the marks for this paper.

1. Study the information below and then answer the questions that follow.

HobbyCraft created 50 jobs when it opened its first branch in Scotland at the Glasgow Fort. HobbyCraft is a private limited company.

Adapted from HobbyCraft website

DO NOT WRITE IN THIS MARGIN

Marks | KU | DM

1. (continued)

(*a*) Suggest and justify **2** reasons why HobbyCraft may have chosen to locate at the Glasgow Fort.

You must give 2 different justifications.

Suggestion 1 ______________________________

Justification ______________________________

____

____

Suggestion 2 ______________________________

Justification ______________________________

____

______________________________ **4**

(*b*) Identify **2** features of a private limited company.

1 ______________________________

____

2 ______________________________

______________________________ **2**

(*c*) Identify **4** steps used in the recruitment and selection process.

1 ______________________________

____

2 ______________________________

____

3 ______________________________

____

4 ______________________________

______________________________ **4**

DO NOT WRITE IN THIS MARGIN

Marks KU DM

2. Aleksi Gorzowski manufactures wooden rocking horses.

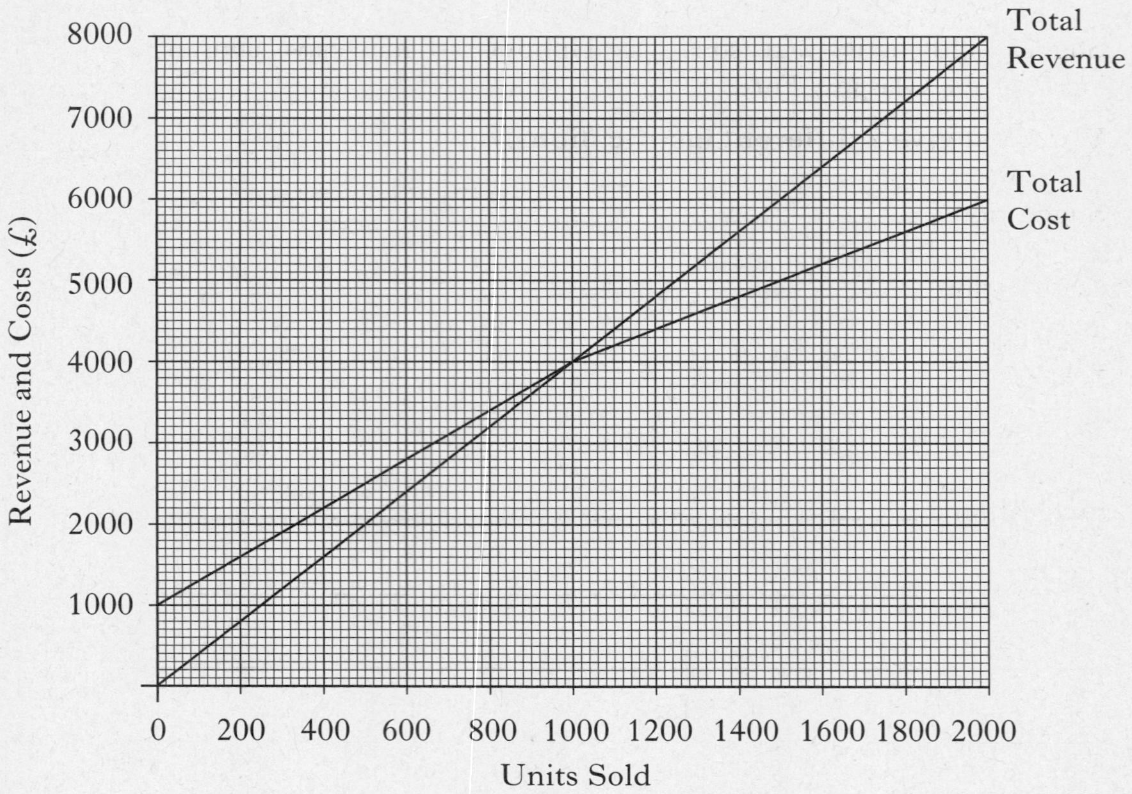

(*a*) Identify from the above graph:

(i) Number of units sold at break-even point;

____

(ii) Total Revenue at break-even point.

____ **2**

(*b*) Identify the following costs as fixed or variable. Put a tick (✓) in the correct box.

	Fixed Cost	Variable Cost
Rent		
Raw Materials		
Insurance		

3

DO NOT WRITE IN THIS MARGIN

Marks KU DM

2. (continued)

(*c*) Aleksi is calculating his costs. Please help him to complete the missing figures. Insert your answers in the table below.

Month	Fixed Cost	Variable Cost	Total Cost
January	£1000	£2500	
February	£1000		£5000
March		£3500	£4500

3

(*d*) Suggest and justify a suitable software application which Aleksi could use to help him calculate the above information.

Software Application ______________________________

Justification ______________________________

______________________________ **2**

[Turn over

DO NOT WRITE IN THIS MARGIN

Marks KU DM

3. **Sales of Games Consoles January 2007**

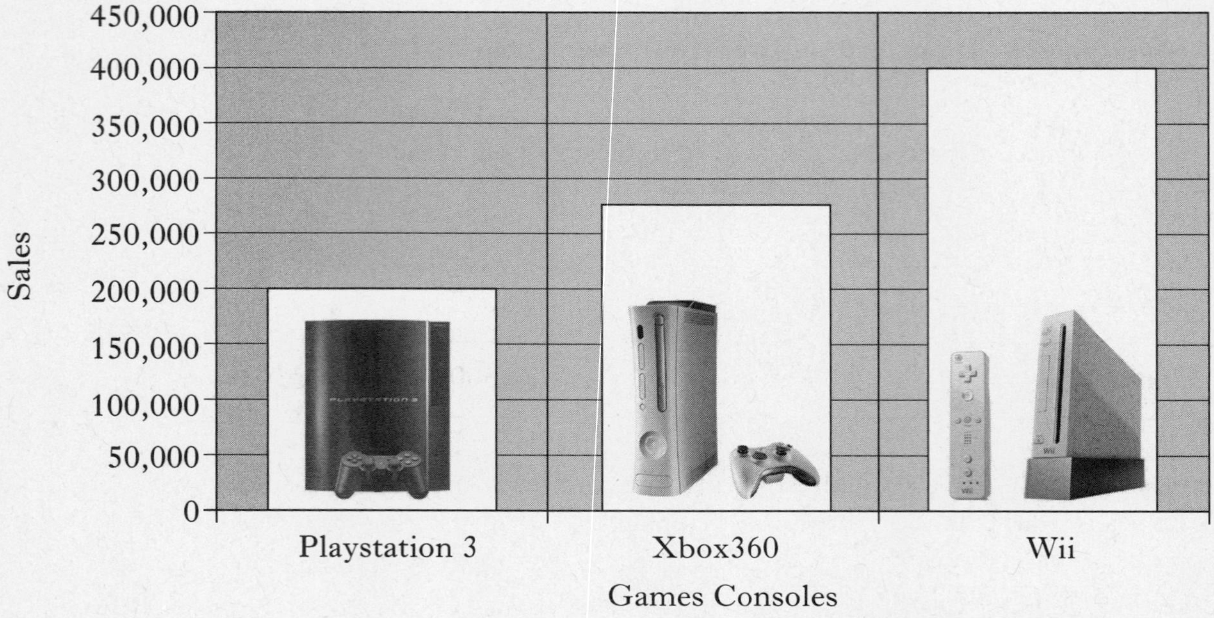

Adapted from CNNMoney.com

In 2007 there was fierce competition in the games console market. Nintendo Wii, Sony Playstation 3 and Microsoft Xbox carried out market research to gain customers.

(*a*) (i) From the diagram above, identify the market leader.

____ **1**

(ii) Suggest **one** reason why it is important to be the market leader.

____

____

____ **1**

DO NOT WRITE IN THIS MARGIN

Marks KU DM

3. (continued)

(*b*) Sony, Microsoft and Nintendo carry out market research.

Identify and describe **one** method of field research and **one** method of desk research.

Field Method ____________________

____

Description ____________________

____

____

Desk Method ____________________

____

Description ____________________

____

____________________ **4**

(*c*) Suggest and justify a pricing policy which could be used by Microsoft.

Pricing Policy ____________________

Justification ____________________

____

____________________ **2**

(*d*) Other than price, suggest **2** ways the games console manufacturers can compete with each other.

Suggestion 1 ____________________

____

Suggestion 2 ____________________

____________________ **2**

[Turn over

DO NOT WRITE IN THIS MARGIN

	Marks	KU	DM

3. (continued)

(*e*) Other than price, describe **2** elements of the marketing mix.

1 ____

____

____

2 ____

____

____ **2**

[Turn over for Question 4 on *Page ten*

DO NOT WRITE IN THIS MARGIN

Marks KU DM

4. Having a business meeting and need sandwiches? Why not get in touch with Beetroot Blue? You can choose from our menu or you can create your own. You order on-line, we prepare your sandwiches and deliver them to you.

Source: www.beetrootblue.com

(*a*) Name and describe a suitable method of production which could be used by Beetroot Blue.

Method of Production ____________________

Description ____________________

____

____________________ 2

(*b*) Suggest **2** advantages to customers of ordering on-line.

1 ____________________

____

2 ____________________

____________________ 2

(*c*) Suggest **one** disadvantage to customers of ordering on-line.

____

____

____________________ 1

DO NOT WRITE IN THIS MARGIN

Marks | KU | DM

4. (continued)

(*d*) Beetroot Blue is involved in both secondary and tertiary sectors of industry. Explain the terms:

Secondary Sector ______________________________

____

____

Tertiary Sector ______________________________

____

______________________________ **2**

[Turn over

DO NOT WRITE IN THIS MARGIN

Marks KU DM

5. Jenny Scott had a dream of one day owning her own business. Jenny felt that there was a gap in the market for fashion accessories and jewellery. Jenny got a loan from the Prince's Trust who asked her for a business plan.
She started her business and called it "Lily".

Source: Determined to Succeed website

(*a*) Give **2** headings contained in a Business Plan.

Heading 1 ______________________________

Heading 2 ______________________________ **2**

(*b*) Suggest **2** aims which Jenny could have for her business.

1 ______________________________

____

2 ______________________________

______________________________ **2**

(*c*) Suggest **2** stakeholders in "Lily" and the interest each stakeholder will have in the business.

Stakeholder 1 ______________________________

Interest ______________________________

____

____

Stakeholder 2 ______________________________

Interest ______________________________

____

______________________________ **4**

DO NOT WRITE IN THIS MARGIN

Marks | KU | DM

5. (continued)

(*d*) "Lily" operates a flat structure. Suggest **one** advantage of this type of structure.

____

____

____ **1**

(*e*) Identify and describe **one** other type of organisation structure.

Type of organisation structure ______________________

____

Description ______________________________________

____

____ **2**

[Turn over

DO NOT WRITE IN THIS MARGIN

Marks | KU | DM

6.

We Save the Children
Will you?

SCHOOLS
aren't for all
children
WE think
they should be
YOU Find out more →

Save the Children exists to just do that—save children. The charity aims to give children a better chance in life by providing food, medicines and education. Marks & Spencer, Next and Virgin are three of the many businesses who have supported the charity.

Source: Adapted from Save the Children website

(*a*) Suggest **one** reason why businesses are keen to support "Save the Children".

____

____

____ **1**

(*b*) Other than business support, suggest **3** ways "Save the Children" can raise finance.

Suggestion 1 ______________________________________

____

Suggestion 2 ______________________________________

____

Suggestion 3 ______________________________________

____ **3**

DO NOT WRITE IN THIS MARGIN

Marks KU DM

6. (continued)

(*c*) "Save the Children" is in the voluntary sector of the economy. Name and describe **2** other sectors of the economy.

Sector ______________________________

Description ______________________________

____

____

Sector ______________________________

Description ______________________________

____

______________________________ **4**

(*d*) Suggest **2** ways "Save the Children" could raise awareness of the charity.

Suggestion 1 ______________________________

____

____

Suggestion 2 ______________________________

____

______________________________ **2**

[*END OF QUESTION PAPER*]

[BLANK PAGE]

STANDARD GRADE | CREDIT

2009

[BLANK PAGE]

C

4200/403

NATIONAL QUALIFICATIONS 2009

TUESDAY, 19 MAY
1.00 PM – 2.30 PM

BUSINESS MANAGEMENT
STANDARD GRADE
Credit Level

1 Read each question carefully.

2 Attempt **all** the questions.

3 All answers are to be written in the answer book provided.

DO NOT WRITE IN THIS MARGIN

KU DM

1.

Ford, a multinational company, has been criticised for its failure to respond to market changes over the years. However, a customer feedback survey has shown that the new versions of its leading cars—the Ka, Focus and Mondeo have been welcomed by customers.

All of the cars have been around for over 10 years—and all have reached the "maturity" stage of the Product Life Cycle. The new versions are just one of the ways Ford has managed to successfully extend the life-cycles of its cars.

(*a*) Describe **2** benefits of being a multinational company. 2

(*b*) (i) Explain the possible consequences to a business of failing to respond to changes in the market. 2

(ii) Explain how a customer feedback survey could be useful in the decision making process for a business. 1

(*c*) Other than new versions of the product, describe and justify **2** ways in which Ford could extend the Product Life Cycle of its cars. 4

(*d*) Suggest and justify **3** ways in which Ford could ensure quality in the production process of its cars. 6

DO NOT WRITE IN THIS MARGIN

	KU	DM

2.

VACANCY

FINANCE MANAGER

CSU Sportswear requires a Finance Manager to run a busy Finance Department for a Scottish chain of 20 branches.

The role will involve:

- preparing Cash Budgets
- preparing Final Accounts
- reviewing monthly performance of branches
- supervising the work of 4 Finance Assistants
- conducting employee appraisals for Finance Assistants

The suitable candidate will have a degree in Finance and at least 2 years experience of working in a similar role.

Please forward your CV
to Mrs Fiona Russell, HR Manager,
CSU Sportswear, Head Office,
20 Argyll Road,
Edinburgh, EH97 8JJ

		KU	DM
(*a*)	Suggest and justify **2** suitable places this vacancy could be advertised to attract the most suitably qualified candidate.		4
(*b*)	(i) Describe the purpose of preparing a Cash Budget.	2	
	(ii) Suggest and justify **2** possible actions that can be taken when problems are identified in the Cash budget.		4
(*c*)	Other than a Cash Budget, identify and describe **2** financial statements that are prepared within the Finance Department.	4	
(*d*)	(i) Describe the purpose of Appraisal.	2	
	(ii) Give **2** benefits to the employee of Appraisal.	2	

[Turn over

DO NOT WRITE IN THIS MARGIN

KU | DM

3.

The Prince's Scottish Youth Business Trust

A young entrepreneur, backed by the Prince's Scottish Youth Business Trust (PSYBT), won a prize at an awards ceremony celebrating innovation. Paul Sommerville's winning idea is a new type of baby monitor which offers a unique way of monitoring the movement, temperature and breathing of babies while they sleep.

His company worked with a team of Scottish designers to come up with a prototype before going into production. Due to the advanced safety features and modern style of the product, there has been considerable interest from manufacturers and retailers worldwide.

(*a*) (i) Explain the term "prototype". **1** (KU)

(ii) Describe **3** stages involved in bringing a new product to market. **3** (KU)

(*b*) (i) Describe **2** risks involved in launching a new product. **2** (KU)

(ii) Suggest how entrepreneurs can reduce risks. **2** (DM)

(*c*) (i) Other than the PSYBT suggest **2** ways in which entrepreneurs can get advice in setting up their business. **2** (DM)

(ii) Explain why the government is keen to support new business start-ups. **2** (KU)

DO NOT WRITE IN THIS MARGIN

	KU	DM

4.

The Harlequin Restaurants empire stared in 1984, when entrepreneurs Charan Gill and his business partner, Gurmail Dhillon purchased the Ashoka West-End Restaurant in Glasgow. Over the next two decades the group grew from strength to strength to become The Harlequin Leisure Group. Harlequin were the first chain of Indian restaurants to introduce a "free-phone-call-centre" to take telephone calls for home deliveries. This has enabled them to build a large database of loyal customers.

In March 2005 Harlequin was sold to the entrepreneur Sanjay Majhu. Plans for the future include the expansion of Ashoka outlets in various food court sites within shopping malls throughout the UK—including Birmingham, London and Belfast.

	Question	KU	DM
(*a*)	Describe the necessary skills and abilities required of an entrepreneur in starting a new business.	4	
(*b*)	Suggest **2** advantages and **2** disadvantages of forming a partnership.	4	
(*c*)	Explain **2** benefits to the business of opening outlets in shopping malls.		2
(*d*)	Other than using the call centre, suggest and justify **2** ways in which Harlequin can use ICT to gain customers throughout the UK.		4

[Turn over for Question 5 on *Page six*

DO NOT WRITE IN THIS MARGIN

	KU	DM
5. A major airline asked ACAS, the industrial dispute peacemaker, to intervene in the row with cabin crew over pay and working conditions. A representative of the Transport General Workers Union (TGWU) also said that there were complaints from staff over an "aggressive management style" being used in the airline. The airline faced a wave of three day strikes after talks broke down.		
(*a*) Explain the role of ACAS in settling industrial disputes in a business.	2	
(*b*) Describe **3** possible consequences to the business if the employees choose to take strike action.		3
(*c*) Identify and describe a management style that could be adopted at an airline company to improve relations with employees.	2	
(*d*) Suggest ways in which an airline company could improve working conditions for their employees.		4

[*END OF QUESTION PAPER*]

STANDARD GRADE | GENERAL

2010

[BLANK PAGE]

FOR OFFICIAL USE

G

KU	DM
Total	

4200/402

NATIONAL QUALIFICATIONS 2010

FRIDAY, 14 MAY
10.20 AM – 11.35 AM

BUSINESS MANAGEMENT
STANDARD GRADE
General Level

Fill in these boxes and read what is printed below.

Full name of centre

Town

Forename(s)

Surname

Date of birth
Day Month Year

Scottish candidate number

Number of seat

1 Read each question carefully.

2 Attempt **all** the questions.

3 All answers are to be written in this answer book.

4 Do **not** write in the margins.

5 Before leaving the examination room you must give this book to the Invigilator. If you do not, you may lose all the marks for this paper.

DO NOT WRITE IN THIS MARGIN

Marks | KU | DM

1. Carla and her brother Fabio always wanted to be entrepreneurs. They decided to go into partnership opening a children's nursery in Peebles. Before going into business they carried out market research. They decided that all communication with parents would be either by e-mail or mobile phone.

(*a*) Suggest **2** skills or qualities that an entrepreneur might have.

1 ______________________________

2 ______________________________ **2**

(*b*) Give **2** advantages of a Partnership.

1 ______________________________

____

2 ______________________________

______________________________ **2**

(*c*) Suggest **one** market segment which Carla and Fabio will target.

______________________________ **1**

(*d*) Suggest **2** reasons why Carla and Fabio carried out market research before starting their business.

1 ______________________________

____

2 ______________________________

______________________________ **2**

DO NOT WRITE IN THIS MARGIN

1. (continued)

	Marks	KU	DM
(*e*) (i) Suggest and justify **one** source of finance for Carla and Fabio when starting their business. Suggestion ______ Justification ______ ______	2		
(ii) Identify **2** sources of advice available to business start-ups. 1 ______ ______ 2 ______ ______	2		
(*f*) (i) Describe **one** problem of using e-mail to communicate. ______ ______ ______	1		
(ii) Suggest **one** advantage of using a mobile phone to communicate. ______ ______	1		

[Turn over

DO NOT WRITE IN THIS MARGIN

2.

Stewarts of Tayside Ltd specialise in growing strawberries and raspberries. All fruit is hand picked using as little mechanisation as possible. The business is committed to caring for the environment.

Adapted from Stewarts of Tayside Ltd website

	Marks	KU	DM
(*a*) Identify the sector of industry which Stewarts of Tayside Ltd operates in. ____________________	1		
(*b*) All fruit is hand picked, using as little mechanisation as possible. Give **one** advantage and **one** disadvantage of mechanisation. Advantage ____________________ ____________________ Disadvantage ____________________ ____________________	2		
(*c*) Suggest **2** channels of distribution which a business could use to get their products to the market. 1 ____________________ ____________________ 2 ____________________ ____________________	2		
(*d*) Give **2** ways Stewarts of Tayside Ltd could care for the environment. 1 ____________________ ____________________ ____________________ 2 ____________________ ____________________ ____________________	2		

[Turn over for Question 3 on *Page six*

DO NOT WRITE IN THIS MARGIN

Marks | KU | DM

3. Marks and Spencer plc believe that people are important to their success and use a Democratic Style of Management.

> YOUR M&S
>
> STORE MANAGER
>
> Required for Argyle Street Branch, Glasgow
>
> Permanent Contract
>
> Salary £35,000 – £45,000
>
> Responsible for managing a team of Section Managers
>
> Apply on-line for application form, job description and person specification
>
> *Adapted from Marks & Spencer website*

(*a*) Suggest **2** places Marks and Spencer plc could advertise this job.

1 ____________________

2 ____________________ **2**

(*b*) Identify **2** features of a public limited company (plc).

1 ____________________

____

2 ____________________

____________________ **2**

DO NOT WRITE IN THIS MARGIN

3. (continued) *Marks* KU DM

(*c*) Explain the term Democratic Style of Management.

____

____

____ **1**

(*d*) Name and describe another style of management.

Style of Management ______________________________

Description ______________________________________

____

____ **2**

(*e*) Identify one feature of a Permanent Contract.

____

____ **1**

(*f*) (i) Identify **3** pieces of information contained in a Job Description.

1 ____

2 ____

3 ____ **3**

(ii) Identify **2** pieces of information contained in a Person Specification.

1 ____

2 ____ **2**

[Turn over

DO NOT WRITE IN THIS MARGIN

Marks | KU | DM

4. Study the Cash Budget below and then answer the questions which follow.

Cash Budget of Shareen Patel

for 3 months January – March 2010

	January (£)	February (£)	March (£)
Opening Balance	1,000	?	3,500
Cash In			
Sales	12,000	11,500	11,000
	13,000	14,500	14,500
Cash Out			
Raw Materials	7,000	8,000	8,500
Wages	1,000	1,000	1,000
Rent	1,200	1,200	1,200
Heating/Lighting/Gas/Telephone	800	800	800
Purchase of new vehicle	0	0	10,000
	10,000	11,000	21,500
Closing Balance	3,000	3,500	(7,000)

(*a*) (i) State the opening balance in February.

____________________ **1**

(ii) Explain what has happened to the closing balance in March.

____________________ **1**

(*b*) Suggest **2** ways Shareen Patel could increase sales.

1 ____________________

____

2 ____________________

____________________ **2**

DO NOT WRITE IN THIS MARGIN

4. (continued)

Marks KU DM

(*c*) Suggest and justify **2** ways Shareen Patel could reduce Cash Out.

You should use a different justification for each suggestion.

Suggestion 1 ______________________________

____

Justification ______________________________

____

____

Suggestion 2 ______________________________

____

Justification ______________________________

____

______________________________ **4**

(*d*) (i) Give **one** reason why Shareen Patel has prepared a Cash Budget.

____

______________________________ **1**

(ii) Suggest a software application that could be used to prepare a Cash Budget and suggest **one** advantage of using this package.

Software application ______________________________

Advantage ______________________________

______________________________ **2**

[Turn over

DO NOT WRITE IN THIS MARGIN

Marks | KU | DM

5. During 2008, discount supermarkets saw sales grow. Aldi, Lidl and Netto saw their market share rise to 6·1%—their best ever result. This trend is set to continue as Aldi and Lidl both have plans to expand across the UK.

Food Market Share of UK Supermarkets

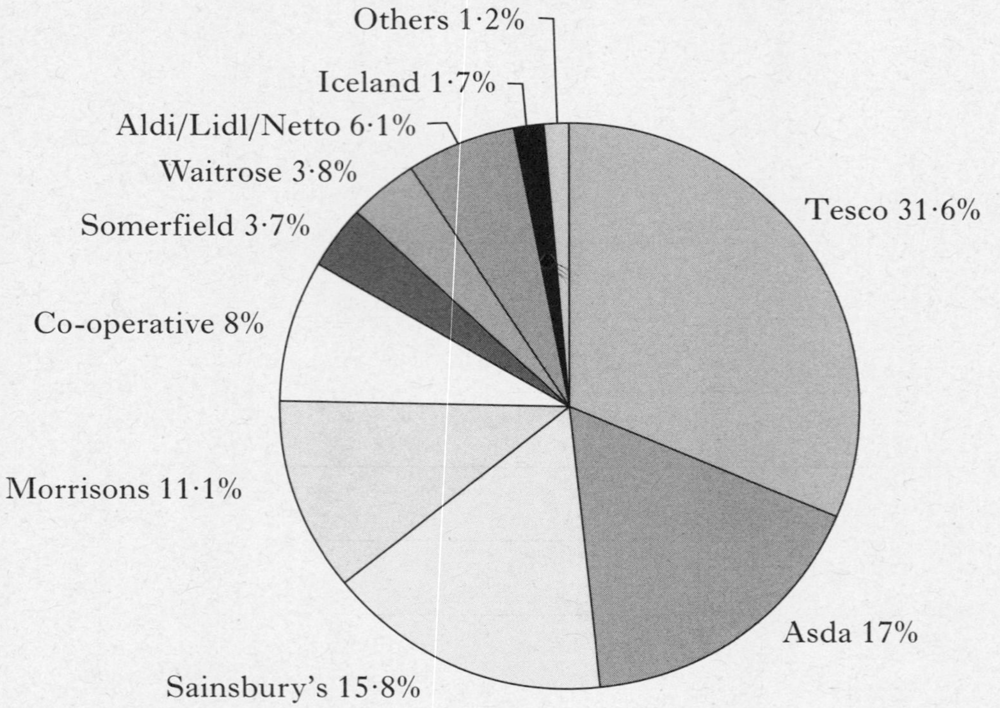

Adapted from www.bbc.co.uk/business website

(*a*) Explain the term market share.

____

____ **1**

(*b*) (i) From the above chart, identify the supermarket with the highest market share.

____ **1**

(ii) From the above chart, identify the market share held by Morrisons.

____ **1**

DO NOT WRITE IN THIS MARGIN

5. (continued)

Marks KU DM

(*c*) Other than price, suggest **3** reasons why people choose to shop in a particular supermarket.

Suggestion 1 ______________________

____

Suggestion 2 ______________________

____

Suggestion 3 ______________________

______________________ **3**

(*d*) Suggest **2** reasons why Aldi and Lidl want to expand across the UK.

1 ______________________

____

2 ______________________

______________________ **2**

[Turn over

DO NOT WRITE IN THIS MARGIN

6.

Coca-Cola

Coca-Cola in East Kilbride has one of the most modern continuous flow bottling plants in the UK. They produce millions of cases of soft drinks a year. As part of their Mission Statement, they always try to satisfy customer's needs, as well as providing a great place for their employees to work.

Adapted from Coca-Cola website

Marks KU DM

(*a*) Explain the term continuous flow production.

____

____ **1**

(*b*) Suggest one advantage and one disadvantage of continuous flow production to Coca-Cola.

(i) Advantage ______________________________

____

____ **1**

(ii) Disadvantage ______________________________

____

____ **1**

(*c*) Explain the purpose of a Mission Statement.

____

____

____ **1**

(*d*) Suggest **2** ways Coca-Cola can satisfy the needs of their customers.

Suggestion 1 ______________________________

____

Suggestion 2 ______________________________

____ **2**

DO NOT WRITE IN THIS MARGIN

6. (continued) *Marks* KU DM

(*e*) Suggest **2** ways a business can motivate its employees.

1 ______________________________

____

2 ______________________________

______________________________ **2**

[*END OF QUESTION PAPER*]

[BLANK PAGE]

STANDARD GRADE | CREDIT

2010

[BLANK PAGE]

C

4200/403

NATIONAL QUALIFICATIONS 2010

FRIDAY, 14 MAY
1.00 PM – 2.30 PM

BUSINESS MANAGEMENT
STANDARD GRADE
Credit Level

1 Read each question carefully.

2 Attempt **all** the questions.

3 All answers are to be written in the answer book provided.

DO NOT WRITE IN THIS MARGIN

	KU	DM

1.

i'm lovin' it®

The "golden arches" of McDonald's are one of the most widely recognised global brands. Driven by changing social trends towards healthier food, McDonald's launched its biggest change in the company's 30 year history—a new menu. McDonald's now provides nutritional information on its full menu to customers in store and via its website.

Restaurants are being redesigned with leather seating and modern styling. McDonald's offers free wi-fi access in over 1,000 restaurants in the UK. McDonald's is constantly looking at ways to improve its customer service. Employee training has always been important—in 2008 McDonald's was given the right to award its own qualifications to employees in the UK.

Question	KU	DM
(*a*) Describe **3** benefits to McDonald's of having a strong brand.	3	
(*b*) Other than social trends, identify and describe **2** external factors that may affect McDonald's.	4	
(*c*) Suggest additional information that McDonald's may display on their website, other than nutritional values of food.		4
(*d*) Describe one method of on-the-job training and one method of off-the-job training.	2	
(*e*) From the case study, identify ways in which McDonald's have improved customer service.		4

DO NOT WRITE IN THIS MARGIN

KU DM

2.

MOON MICROSYSTEMS LTD—CUSTOM BUILT PCs

Dan Mooney set up Moon Microsystems in a small shop in Perth. As his business grew he opened a further 9 shops throughout Scotland, he now employs 45 staff. Dan prides himself on being a good manager. He has a flat management structure with all store managers reporting directly to him and all technicians and sales staff are on the same level. He is thinking of offering flexible working to employees.

As each computer is custom-built to order, just-in-time manufacturing is employed. Moon Microsystems has monthly meetings between branches.

(*a*) (i) Describe **2** advantages and **2** disadvantages of operating a flat management structure. **4** (KU)

(ii) Explain the term "span of control". **1** (KU)

(*b*) Describe **3** skills or qualities of an effective manager. **3** (KU)

(*c*) Suggest **4** examples of flexible working methods that could be offered in Moon Microsystems Ltd. **4** (DM)

(*d*) Give **2** benefits to Moon Microsystems of using just-in-time manufacturing. **2** (KU)

(*e*) Suggest and justify **2** ways in which Moon Microsystems could use ICT for communication. **4** (DM)

[Turn over

DO NOT WRITE IN THIS MARGIN

KU DM

3. Danika Jansa, a fashion designer, has prepared her first set of accounts and is concerned about her profits.

DANIKA'S DESIGNS

Trading and Profit and Loss A/C for year ending 31/12/09

	£	£
Sales		80,000
Less: Cost of Sales		
Opening Stock	15,000	
Add: Purchases	15,000	
	30,000	
Less: Closing Stock	10,000	20,000
GROSS PROFIT		60,000
Less: Expenses		
Wages	28,000	
Administration	10,000	
Gas & Electricity	8,000	
Telephone	2,000	48,000
NET PROFIT		12,000

Balance sheet as at 31/12/09

	£	£
Fixed Assets		25,000
Current Assets		
Stock	15,000	
Debtors	10,000	
Bank	8,000	
	33,000	
Current Liabilities		
Creditors	8,000	25,000
Capital Employed		50,000
Financed by:		
Capital at Start		15,000
Add: Net Profit		12,000
Bank Loan		23,000
Capital at End		50,000

(*a*) Describe the difference between Gross Profit and Net Profit. 2

(*b*) Identify and give the formula for one financial ratio that can be prepared from the Trading, Profit and Loss Account. 2

(*c*) Describe **2** decisions that Danika could make to improve the Net Profit. 2

(*d*) (i) Explain the term Fixed Assets. 2

(ii) Give one example of a Fixed Asset that Danika might have in the business. 1

(*e*) Other than Danika, suggest another stakeholder that might be interested in the final accounts. Give one influence this stakeholder may have on the business. 2

DO NOT WRITE IN THIS MARGIN

KU DM

4.

The **co-operative**

Somerfield

The Co-operative Group has increased its market share in Scotland after snapping up rival food chain Somerfield, making it the market leader in local convenience stores.

The Chief Executive of the Co-op stated that convenience stores were already winning customers from their larger superstore rivals as a result of higher fuel costs persuading more people to shop locally. However, there is fierce competition in this market with rivals such as Spar and Londis holding prime locations in Scottish towns and cities.

(*a*) Explain the term Market Leader. **1**

(*b*) (i) From the Case Study identify the method of integration that has taken place. Give **one** possible disadvantage of this integration. **2**

(ii) Identify and describe another method of integration. **2**

(*c*) Give reasons why customers may prefer to use a local shop rather than a superstore. **3**

(*d*) Identify **3** factors influencing the location of a business. **3**

(*e*) Suggest and justify **2** ways in which the Co-op can compete with its rivals. **4**

[Turn over for Question 5 on *Page six*

DO NOT WRITE IN THIS MARGIN

KU DM

5.

Nintendo has continued to dominate the games market. Nintendo are a market led business.

The success of the innovative Wii product has provided an unexpected boost to Nintendo. The Wii Sports and Wii Fit encouraged gamers to be more active. The DS enabled Nintendo to target both older consumers and females too, traditionally excluded from the gaming market.

Demand for the Nintendo Wii has been incredible—in December 2007 the company failed to produce enough consoles to keep up with consumer demand—stores ran out weeks before Christmas.

(*a*) (i) Explain the difference between market led and product led business. 2

(ii) Give **one** advantage and **one** disadvantage to a business of adopting a market led approach. 2

(*b*) Suggest, describe and justify an appropriate pricing strategy for Nintendo's games consoles. 3

(*c*) In December 2007 production did not meet consumption levels. Describe ways in which Nintendo could have avoided this problem. 2

[*END OF QUESTION PAPER*]

[BLANK PAGE]

[BLANK PAGE]

[BLANK PAGE]

[BLANK PAGE]

Acknowledgements

Permission has been sought from all relevant copyright holders and Bright Red Publishing is grateful for the use of the following:
An extract adapted from www.mybusiness.co.uk (2006 General page 2);
The Forever Natural logo, reproduced with permission of Forever Natural (2006 General page 2);
Data is adapted from www.scotland.gov.uk © Crown Copyright. Reproduced under the terms of the Click-Use Licence (2006 General page 4);
The Murray and Murray Ltd logo and picture. Reproduced with permission of Murray and Murray Ltd (2006 General page 6);
An article adapted from 'Murray & Murray: Scottish Agenda' by Robert Ballantyne, from The Sunday Times, 3 July 2005 © Robert Ballantyne/The Sunday Times, 03 July 2005 (2006 General page 6);
An article and picture adapted from www.innocentdrinks.co.uk (2006 General page 8);
A picture, the Odeon name and information are adapted from www.odeoncinemas.co.uk from 2006. Reproduced by permission of ODEON. Please note that this image is from 2006 and not representative of the current ODEON logo or website (2006 General page 10);
A photograph of a Zara shop © Inditex (2006 Credit page 2);
An article adapted from 'The Future of Fast Fashion' taken from 'The Economist' Jun 16, 2005 © The Economist Newspaper Limited, London 2005 (2006 Credit page 2);
An extract adapted from The Scotsman, 5 and 6 September 2005 © The Scotsman Publications Ltd (2006 Credit page 5);
A logo and article are adapted from www.greggs.co.uk © Greggs plc (2007 General page 2);
A logo, picture and article are adapted from www.islandbakery.co.uk. Reproduced with permission of Island Bakery Organics (2007 General page 6);
An image of an iPod and iPod Nano © Apple Computer Ltd (2007 General page 8);
A photograph and article are adapted from www.lochfyne.com © Loch Fyne Oysters Ltd (2007 General page 10);
A logo and article adapted from www.princes-trust.org.uk. Reproduced by permission of The Prince's Trust (2007 General page 12);
A logo and article adapted from www.mackies.co.uk. Reproduced with permission of Mackie's Limited (2007 Credit page 2);
The amazon.com logo © amazon.com, Inc. (2007 Credit page 3);
An extract adapted from the article 'Grampian moves pig processing' by Fordyce Maxwell, taken from The Scotsman, Saturday 16 April 2005 © The Scotsman Publications Ltd (2007 Credit page 6);
The Grampian Country Food Group logo © VION Food Group (2007 Credit page 6);
An extract and image adapted from the Walkers Shortbread Ltd Website © Walkers Shortbread Ltd (2008 General page 2);
Text and picture adapted from Spar Website © Spar UK Limited (2008 General page 10);
Text and picture adapted from Dobbies website © Dobbies Garden Centre Plc (2008 General page 12);
Text and a picture of Tunnocks biscuits taken from www.tunnock.co.uk, reproduced by permission of Thomas Tunnock Limited (2008 Credit page 2);
Text and picture taken from House of Fraser website. Reproduced by permission of House of Fraser (2008 Credit page 3);
Extract adapted from an article by Paul Drury of Media Now, as used on the BBC Scotland website on 30 August 2006. Reproduced with permission of Paul Drury (2008 Credit page 4);
The logo for Aldi © Aldi Stores (2008 Credit page 6);
The logo for Lidl. Reproduced by permission of Lidl UK (2008 Credit page 6);
Text taken from an article in Scotland on Sunday, 6 August 2006 by William Lyons. Published by Scotland on Sunday © The Scotsman Publications Ltd (2008 Credit page 6);
An extract adapted from HobbyCraft website. Reproduced with permission of HobbyCraft Group Limited (2009 General page 2);
An image © Glasgow Fort Shopping Park, Junction 10 M8 (2009 General page 2);
The graph 'Sales of Games Consoles January 2007' adapted from CNNMoney.com (2009 General page 6);
An image of an Xbox 360. Reproduced with permission of Microsoft (2009 General page 6);
An image of a Nintendo Wii © Nintendo (2009 General page 6);
An image of a Playstation 3 © Sony Computer Entertainment Inc (2009 General page 6);
An extract and image adapted from www.beetroot blue.com © Beetroot Blue (2009 General page 10);
An extract and image adapted from the Determined to Succeed website © Crown Copyright. Reproduced under the terms of the Click-Use Licence (2009 General page 12);
An extract and image adapted from Save the Children website. Reproduced with permission (2009 General page 14);
The Cradlesafe logo. Reproduced by permission of Cradlesafe (2009 Credit page 2);
The Ford logo. Reproduced with permission of Ford (2009 Credit page 2);
The logo for The Prince's Scottish Youth Business Trust. Reproduced with permission (2009 Credit page 2);
An image and photograph from The Harlequin Restaurant Group website © Harlequin Restaurants (2009 Credit page 5);
An extract and images adapted from Stewarts of Tayside Ltd website © Stewarts of Tayside Ltd (2010 General page 4);

The Marks & Spencer logo and text adapted from the Marks & Spencer website © Marks and Spencer plc (2010 General page 6);
The Coca-Cola logo and text adapted from the Coca-Cola website © Coca-Cola (2010 General page 12);
The McDonald's logo and photograph of a McDonald's restaurant. Used with permission from McDonald's Restaurants Limited (2010 Credit page 2);
The logos for The Co-operative & Somerfield and photograph of a Co-operative store © The Co-operative Group (2010 Credit page 5);
Two images of a Nintendo Wii and Nintendo DS © Nintendo (2010 Credit page 6).